Goatia Demons Disco Magick

S ROB

DEDICATION

I dedicate this book to my mother and father.

CONTENTS

ACKNOWLEDGMENTS

I acknowledge the existence of real magick.

Chapter 1 Baal for protection

The magick you will learn in this book is a fusion of satanic magick and music. I feel that for too long have these two subjects remained largely separate. In fact, I have written books on music and occultism before but not a lot. The truth is that the music helps to empower the magick. You may wonder why disco music and I would say because disco music lends a special quality that I find good when we are working magick. Goatia demons are a different sort of demonic creatures because they are those which come from a particular occult tradition. However, to summon these demons: many in fact are devils: we will be using the power of Leviathan a potent devil whose mouth is quite literally the Mouth of Hell itself. This means that Leviathan can open it's mouth and we summon a demon: or devil: through, tell it what we wish it to do and then send it back again and at the end get Leviathan to close it's mouth once more. However don't think that all you need do is to say some words to disco music because there is one more thing, you must strongly will this magick to work: the reason for this is that in reality it is the power of your own will that is the true fuel for this magick.

As well as using Leviathan you will also be using the devil named Baal. It is said that Baal has three heads: one of a man, one of a toad and one of a cat. He has many estates and is the first king of Hell: there being quite a few. In the goatia structure Lucifer the actual Devil is styled more as a god than as someone you can contact. The first magick will be to get protection from Baal with the assistance of Leviathan to summon him. This magick follows now.

Baal magick for protection

(You will need the music Disco Inferno by the Tramps ready to start: any adverts before music should be listened to already)

MUSIC PLAYING: DISCO INFERNO MOVE TO THE MUSIC
AS YOU SAY THESE WORDS

Leviathan you are a powerful devil a great monster and your mouth
is the very mouth of Hell itself. Leviathan powerful devil and I ask
that you open your mouth that is the very mouth of Hell itself: The
Gates of Hell, the Hell Mouth. Leviathan open the Hell Mouth, the
Hell Mouth: The Hell Mouth opens it is open. I summon through
the Hell Mouth the first King of Hell Baal, he with three heads: one
of a man, one of a toad and one of a cat: he with two estates and
commander of 66 legions. Baal come through the gates: Baal
comes through the gates and is here with me. Baal first King of
Hell I ask that you make it so that your 66 legions protect me from
any harm whatsoever so that nothing harmful can happen to me and
this is what I ask of you. Baal the first King of Hell agrees to help
and departs back through the Mouth of Hell. Leviathan you are a
powerful devil a great monster and your mouth is the very mouth of

3

Hell itself. Leviathan powerful devil and I ask that you close your mouth that is the very mouth of Hell itself: The Gates of Hell, the Hell Mouth. Leviathan close the Hell Mouth, the Hell Mouth: The Hell Mouth closes it is closed. So it is and will be.

END MUSIC

You will now be working more magick with Baal and this is to protect an area. In fact, this magick will protect both the area this magick is performed in and anything or anyone within it. I also wish you to understand the importance of protecting both the area or areas you spend time in and yourself and this means at least protective magick for you and for your home: the latter follows.

Baal magick to protect an area

(You will need the music Stayin Alive by the Bee Gees ready to start: any adverts before music should be listened to already)

MUSIC PLAYING: STAYIN ALIVE MOVE TO THE MUSIC AS YOU SAY THESE WORDS

Leviathan you are a powerful devil a great monster and your mouth is the very mouth of Hell itself. Leviathan powerful devil and I ask that you open your mouth that is the very mouth of Hell itself: The Gates of Hell, the Hell Mouth. Leviathan open the Hell Mouth, the Hell Mouth: The Hell Mouth opens it is open. I summon through the Hell Mouth the first King of Hell Baal, he with three heads: one of a man, one of a toad and one of a cat: he with two estates and commander of 66 legions. Baal come through the gates: Baal comes through the gates and is here with me. Baal first King of Hell I ask that you make it so that your 66 legions protect this place and all within it from any harm and from all attacks of any kind and variety and this is what I ask of you. Baal the first King of Hell agrees to help and departs back through the Mouth of Hell. Leviathan you are a powerful devil a great monster and your mouth is the very mouth of Hell itself. Leviathan powerful devil and I ask that you close your mouth that is the very mouth of Hell itself: The Gates of Hell, the Hell Mouth. Leviathan close the Hell Mouth, the Hell Mouth: The Hell Mouth closes it is closed. So it is and will be. END MUSIC

It seems to me that we need to think on what magick we can do to help our family because unless you are split what happens to them affects you; even if not directly. I feel therefore that for many forms of families we need protective magick and this is what I offer now.

Baal magick to protect all family

(You will need the music YMCA by the Village People ready to start: any adverts before music should be listened to already)

MUSIC PLAYING: YMCA MOVE TO THE MUSIC AS YOU SAY THESE WORDS

Leviathan you are a powerful devil a great monster and your mouth is the very mouth of Hell itself. Leviathan powerful devil and I ask that you open your mouth that is the very mouth of Hell itself: The Gates of Hell, the Hell Mouth. Leviathan open the Hell Mouth, the Hell Mouth: The Hell Mouth opens it is open. I summon through the Hell Mouth the first King of Hell Baal, he with three heads: one of a man, one of a toad and one of a cat: he with two estates and commander of 66 legions. Baal come through the gates: Baal comes through the gates and is here with me. Baal first King of Hell I ask that you make it so that your 66 legions protect my family from any harm whatsoever so that nothing harmful can happen to them and this is what I ask of you. Baal the first King of Hell agrees to help and departs back through the Mouth of Hell. Leviathan you are a powerful devil a great monster and your mouth is the very mouth of Hell itself. Leviathan powerful devil and I ask that you close your mouth that is the very mouth of Hell itself: The

Gates of Hell, the Hell Mouth. Leviathan close the Hell Mouth, the Hell Mouth: The Hell Mouth closes it is closed. So it is and will be. END MUSIC

You have in fact reached out to magick and as it does it does not leave your hand floating but reaches back to help you. Magick can be the most helpful force of all. But this magick also helps you understand that there exists different planes of reality and different forms of life, different beings unlike and yet also quite like us. We should not think that in life when we come upon something helpless that it is necessarily helpless; because magick can help us. However, you have finished the magick in the last chapter and so you have space to grow as you proceed through the rest of the book.

Chapter 2 Baal attack magick

This chapter is about attacking: getting the first king of Hell and his 66 legions to attack for you. I understand that in life we sometimes need to attack and so do use the magick here when you feel the time is appropriate. This is good because this whole book is really about choice and I firmly believe that slavery exists and I feel that once after hypnotizing kidnappers and walking free from a fake hotel designed to kidnap people that if I had gotten into the car that was provided that I would most likely as not be a slave. I therefore wish to free all the slaves.

Baal magick to attack a chosen person

(You will need the music I feel good by James Brown ready to start: any adverts before music should be listened to already)

MUSIC PLAYING: I FEEL GOOD MOVE TO THE MUSIC AS YOU SAY THESE WORDS

Leviathan you are a powerful devil a great monster and your mouth is the very mouth of Hell itself. Leviathan powerful devil and I ask that you open your mouth that is the very mouth of Hell itself: The Gates of Hell, the Hell Mouth. Leviathan open the Hell Mouth, the Hell Mouth: The Hell Mouth opens it is open. I summon through the Hell Mouth the first King of Hell Baal, he with three heads: one of a man, one of a toad and one of a cat: he with two estates and commander of 66 legions. Baal come through the gates: Baal comes through the gates and is here with me. Baal first King of Hell I ask that you make it so that your 66 legions attack <u>state name of chosen person</u> and this is what I ask of you. Baal the first King of Hell agrees to help and departs back through the Mouth of Hell. Leviathan you are a powerful devil a great monster and your mouth is the very mouth of Hell itself. Leviathan powerful devil and I ask that you close your mouth that is the very mouth of Hell itself: The Gates of Hell, the Hell Mouth. Leviathan close the Hell Mouth, the

Hell Mouth: The Hell Mouth closes it is closed. So it is and will be.

END MUSIC

This magick is to disembowel a person of your choosing. To be honest I would work this magick and graciously accept whatever affect on the target person you get. However sometimes we should go all out and work magick that is as powerful as we can and for as much as we can think of. To disembowel someone through magick use what follows.

Baal magick to disembowel a chosen person

(You will need the music Boogie Wonderland by Earth, Wind and Fire, ready to start: any adverts before music should be listened to already)

MUSIC PLAYING: BOOGIE WONDERLAND MOVE TO THE MUSIC AS YOU SAY THESE WORDS

Leviathan you are a powerful devil a great monster and your mouth is the very mouth of Hell itself. Leviathan powerful devil and I ask that you open your mouth that is the very mouth of Hell itself: The Gates of Hell, the Hell Mouth. Leviathan open the Hell Mouth, the Hell Mouth: The Hell Mouth opens it is open. I summon through the Hell Mouth the first King of Hell Baal, he with three heads: one of a man, one of a toad and one of a cat: he with two estates and commander of 66 legions. Baal come through the gates: Baal comes through the gates and is here with me. Baal first King of Hell I ask that you make it so that your 66 legions will disembowel state name of chosen person and this is what I ask of you. Baal the first King of Hell agrees to help and departs back through the Mouth of Hell. Leviathan you are a powerful devil a great monster and your mouth is the very mouth of Hell itself. Leviathan powerful devil and I ask that you close your mouth that is the very mouth of Hell itself: The Gates of Hell, the Hell Mouth. Leviathan close the Hell Mouth, the Hell Mouth: The Hell Mouth closes it is closed. So it is and will be.

END MUSIC

The fact is that we are better off with our enemies dead than alive and although these curses that follow may not actually kill it is perfectly possible that they will. However, without enemies our lives are better than they are with them. I also feel I should remind you that this magick isn't a shopping list, it must be spoken and performed while willing magick to be done.

Baal magick to attack all enemies

(You will need the music Living in America by James Brown, ready to start: any adverts before music should be listened to already)

MUSIC PLAYING: LIVING IN AMERICA MOVE TO THE MUSIC AS YOU SAY THESE WORDS

Leviathan you are a powerful devil a great monster and your mouth is the very mouth of Hell itself. Leviathan powerful devil and I ask that you open your mouth that is the very mouth of Hell itself: The Gates of Hell, the Hell Mouth. Leviathan open the Hell Mouth, the Hell Mouth: The Hell Mouth opens it is open. I summon through the Hell Mouth the first King of Hell Baal, he with three heads: one of a man, one of a toad and one of a cat: he with two estates and commander of 66 legions. Baal come through the gates: Baal comes through the gates and is here with me. Baal first King of Hell I ask that you make it so that your 66 legions attack all my enemies and this is what I ask of you. Baal the first King of Hell agrees to help and departs back through the Mouth of Hell. Leviathan you are a powerful devil a great monster and your mouth is the very mouth of Hell itself. Leviathan powerful devil and I ask that you close your mouth that is the very mouth of Hell itself: The Gates of Hell, the Hell Mouth. Leviathan close the Hell Mouth, the

14

Hell Mouth: The Hell Mouth closes it is closed. So it is and will be.

END MUSIC

Have you ever wanted to hang someone? I know and I love you for it. I feel that having this power is a positive thing and so do work what magick you can and you will discover that it will be helpful to you. However, if there really isn't anyone you wish to hang you could skip this part or perhaps find the details of some dictator you can hang instead: hanging dictators is fun even when it doesn't work fully.

Baal magick to hang a chosen person

(You will need the music Rasputin by Boney M, ready to start: any adverts before music should be listened to already)

MUSIC PLAYING: RASPUTIN MOVE TO THE MUSIC AS YOU SAY THESE WORDS

Leviathan you are a powerful devil a great monster and your mouth is the very mouth of Hell itself. Leviathan powerful devil and I ask that you open your mouth that is the very mouth of Hell itself: The Gates of Hell, the Hell Mouth. Leviathan open the Hell Mouth, the Hell Mouth: The Hell Mouth opens it is open. I summon through the Hell Mouth the first King of Hell Baal, he with three heads: one of a man, one of a toad and one of a cat: he with two estates and commander of 66 legions. Baal come through the gates: Baal comes through the gates and is here with me. Baal first King of Hell I ask that you make it so that your 66 legions hang <u>state name of chosen person</u> by the neck until they are dead. and this is what I ask of you. Baal the first King of Hell agrees to help and departs back through the Mouth of Hell. Leviathan you are a powerful devil a great monster and your mouth is the very mouth of Hell itself. Leviathan powerful devil and I ask that you close your mouth that is the very mouth of Hell itself: The Gates of Hell, the Hell

16

Mouth. Leviathan close the Hell Mouth, the Hell Mouth: The Hell Mouth closes it is closed. So it is and will be.

END MUSIC

By now you have gained some idea as to how these demonic beings are used for magick and the extra power that disco music adds. In fact, I would say that disco is a powerful force to add to this magick. But most of all I don't want you to feel defenseless in a hostile world: I want you to be able to be hostile also. In many ways it makes me wonder why the military has conventional armies when surely it would be more productive to have armies of occultists and let the rival sides shout it out with spells and other forms of magick for all time if necessary. I suppose the difference is that in war a strategy may cause a last punch whereas occultism is very much like some martial arts in that there is no last punch; every strike is done while thinking that a follow up punch will be required. In magick when we aim to hurt or kill another, we use magick and yet even if we use as many entities together as we can: which I do on occasions: we also are thinking that if it doesn't work, we attack again. So use what magick is needed and follow up if needed to win.

Chapter 3 Vine and the past, present and future

You will now be learning to work magick with the demon Vine. Vine is said to look like a lion holding a snake riding upon a black horse. Vine has many powers and among them is that he can tell the past, present and the future, can create storms and can bring down walls and buildings. However, his 36 legions of demons also gives him some power over violence also. I will now offer the method of working magick to know the past.

Vine magick to get knowledge of the past that will help you

(You will need the music Celebration by Kool and the Gang, ready to start: any adverts before music should be listened to already)

MUSIC PLAYING: CELEBRATION MOVE TO THE MUSIC AS YOU SAY THESE WORDS

Leviathan you are a powerful devil a great monster and your mouth

is the very mouth of Hell itself. Leviathan powerful devil and I ask

that you open your mouth that is the very mouth of Hell itself: The

Gates of Hell, the Hell Mouth. Leviathan open the Hell Mouth, the

Hell Mouth: The Hell Mouth opens it is open. I summon through

the Hell Mouth the King and Earl and of Hell, Vine, he who is the

lion holding the snake, while riding a black horse, commander of

36 legions of demons. Vine come through the gates: Vine comes

through the gates and is here with me. Vine King of Hell I ask that

you make it so that your 36 legions give knowledge of the past that

will help me and this is what I ask of you. Vine King of Hell agrees

to help and departs back through the Mouth of Hell. Leviathan you

are a powerful devil a great monster and your mouth is the very

mouth of Hell itself. Leviathan powerful devil and I ask that you

close your mouth that is the very mouth of Hell itself: The Gates of

Hell, the Hell Mouth. Leviathan close the Hell Mouth, the Hell

Mouth: The Hell Mouth closes it is closed. So it is and will be.

END MUSIC

Knowing the future: even part of it: helps us greatly. Indeed, this is why this following magick exists because while the last concentrated on useful knowledge of the past this magick relies on useful knowledge of the future. However, do remember that for this magick to work you must wish it to be so as you perform it. But also, do look out for strange events that spell out the future and also knowledge that simply comes to you about the future.

Vine magick to get knowledge of the future that will help you

(You will need the music Play that Funky Music by Wild Cherry, ready to start: any adverts before music should be listened to already)

MUSIC PLAYING: PLAY THAT FUNKY MUSIC MOVE TO THE MUSIC AS YOU SAY THESE WORDS

Leviathan you are a powerful devil a great monster and your mouth is the very mouth of Hell itself. Leviathan powerful devil and I ask that you open your mouth that is the very mouth of Hell itself: The Gates of Hell, the Hell Mouth. Leviathan open the Hell Mouth, the Hell Mouth: The Hell Mouth opens it is open. I summon through the Hell Mouth the King and Earl and of Hell, Vine, he who is the lion holding the snake, while riding a black horse, commander of 36 legions of demons. Vine come through the gates: Vine comes through the gates and is here with me. Vine King of Hell I ask that you make it so that your 36 legions give knowledge of the future that will help me and this is what I ask of you. Vine King of Hell agrees to help and departs back through the Mouth of Hell. Leviathan you are a powerful devil a great monster and your mouth is the very mouth of Hell itself. Leviathan powerful devil and I ask that you close your mouth that is the very mouth of Hell itself: The Gates of Hell, the Hell Mouth. Leviathan close the Hell Mouth, the

Hell Mouth: The Hell Mouth closes it is closed. So it is and will be.

END MUSIC

Some knowledge is useful to gain because it is hidden. The fact is that hidden knowledge is often helpful when gained because others do not have it. However, do not be rush to act upon any knowledge gained because acting on such hidden knowledge often requires great wisdom of the sort that only time may bestow.

Vine magick to get hidden knowledge that will help you

(You will need the music Disco Inferno by The Trammps, ready to start: any adverts before music should be listened to already)

MUSIC PLAYING: DISCO INFERNO MOVE TO THE MUSIC AS YOU SAY THESE WORDS

Leviathan you are a powerful devil a great monster and your mouth is the very mouth of Hell itself. Leviathan powerful devil and I ask that you open your mouth that is the very mouth of Hell itself: The

Gates of Hell, the Hell Mouth. Leviathan open the Hell Mouth, the

Hell Mouth: The Hell Mouth opens it is open. I summon through

the Hell Mouth the King and Earl and of Hell, Vine, he who is the

lion holding the snake, while riding a black horse, commander of

36 legions of demons. Vine come through the gates: Vine comes

through the gates and is here with me. Vine King of Hell I ask that

you make it so that your 36 legions give hidden knowledge that

will help you and this is what I ask of you. Vine King of Hell

agrees to help and departs back through the Mouth of Hell.

Leviathan you are a powerful devil a great monster and your mouth

is the very mouth of Hell itself. Leviathan powerful devil and I ask

that you close your mouth that is the very mouth of Hell itself: The

Gates of Hell, the Hell Mouth. Leviathan close the Hell Mouth, the

Hell Mouth: The Hell Mouth closes it is closed. So it is and will be.

END MUSIC

People hide elements of their past and do so without thinking much about it. The truth is that most people have hidden things in their past. It would also be a lie to say that people do not judge us through our past because they do and so events by us or others to us can haunt us for a long time. Magick to know a person's past follows.

Vine magick to know the past of a chosen person

(You will need the music Stayin Alive by the Bee Gees, ready to start: any adverts before music should be listened to already)

MUSIC PLAYING: STAYIN ALIVE MOVE TO THE MUSIC AS YOU SAY THESE WORDS

Leviathan you are a powerful devil a great monster and your mouth is the very mouth of Hell itself. Leviathan powerful devil and I ask that you open your mouth that is the very mouth of Hell itself: The Gates of Hell, the Hell Mouth. Leviathan open the Hell Mouth, the

Hell Mouth: The Hell Mouth opens it is open. I summon through the Hell Mouth the King and Earl and of Hell, Vine, he who is the lion holding the snake, while riding a black horse, commander of 36 legions of demons. Vine come through the gates: Vine comes through the gates and is here with me. Vine King of Hell I ask that you make it so that your 36 legions help me to get knowledge of the past of <u>state name of chosen person</u> and this is what I ask of you. Vine King of Hell agrees to help and departs back through the Mouth of Hell. Leviathan you are a powerful devil a great monster and your mouth is the very mouth of Hell itself. Leviathan powerful devil and I ask that you close your mouth that is the very mouth of Hell itself: The Gates of Hell, the Hell Mouth. Leviathan close the Hell Mouth, the Hell Mouth: The Hell Mouth closes it is closed. So it is and will be.

END MUSIC

You have now come to a point where you have an understanding of Vine and how to use this demonic being for magick. I understand that I must teach you more but still what you have is both strong and powerful magick; a good combination. However, what you have achieved is a personal achievement and should be seen as such. In fact, I want you to know that I am proud of you for what you have achieved so far. More is to come and I am sure you will also do well at this magick too.

Chapter 4 Vine and hidden knowledge

The magick you will now learn is for you to gain knowledge that will help you gain in power. I wish you to know however that there are many varieties of power and this magick and I myself will be happy if you receive any of these. Power makes everything is life much easier and this is one reason to have it.

Vine magick to learn hidden knowledge that will help you gain in power

(You will need the music Rasputin by Boney M, ready to start: any adverts before music should be listened to already)

MUSIC PLAYING: RASPUTIN MOVE TO THE MUSIC AS YOU SAY THESE WORDS

Leviathan you are a powerful devil a great monster and your mouth is the very mouth of Hell itself. Leviathan powerful devil and I ask that you open your mouth that is the very mouth of Hell itself: The

Gates of Hell, the Hell Mouth. Leviathan open the Hell Mouth, the Hell Mouth: The Hell Mouth opens it is open. I summon through the Hell Mouth the King and Earl and of Hell, Vine, he who is the lion holding the snake, while riding a black horse, commander of 36 legions of demons. Vine come through the gates: Vine comes through the gates and is here with me. Vine King of Hell I ask that you make it so that your 36 legions give hidden knowledge that will help me gain in power and this is what I ask of you. Vine King of Hell agrees to help and departs back through the Mouth of Hell. Leviathan you are a powerful devil a great monster and your mouth is the very mouth of Hell itself. Leviathan powerful devil and I ask that you close your mouth that is the very mouth of Hell itself: The Gates of Hell, the Hell Mouth. Leviathan close the Hell Mouth, the Hell Mouth: The Hell Mouth closes it is closed. So it is and will be. END MUSIC

Being wealthy is better than being poor, or even moderately well off. I will also say that this following magick therefore is important because this is what it helps you achieve; to become wealthier. However, this magick is for you to gain in the knowledge you need to become wealthier. It is said that knowledge is power and so let's make this even stronger by making sure you get just the right knowledge you need.

Vine magick to get hidden knowledge that will help you become wealthier

(You will need the music I will Survive by Gloria Gaynor, ready to start: any adverts before music should be listened to already)

MUSIC PLAYING: I WILL SURVIVE MOVE TO THE MUSIC AS YOU SAY THESE WORDS

Leviathan you are a powerful devil a great monster and your mouth is the very mouth of Hell itself. Leviathan powerful devil and I ask

that you open your mouth that is the very mouth of Hell itself: The Gates of Hell, the Hell Mouth. Leviathan open the Hell Mouth, the Hell Mouth: The Hell Mouth opens it is open. I summon through the Hell Mouth the King and Earl and of Hell, Vine, he who is the lion holding the snake, while riding a black horse, commander of 36 legions of demons. Vine come through the gates: Vine comes through the gates and is here with me. Vine King of Hell I ask that you make it so that your 36 legions give hidden knowledge that will help me become wealthier and this is what I ask of you. Vine King of Hell agrees to help and departs back through the Mouth of Hell. Leviathan you are a powerful devil a great monster and your mouth is the very mouth of Hell itself. Leviathan powerful devil and I ask that you close your mouth that is the very mouth of Hell itself: The Gates of Hell, the Hell Mouth. Leviathan close the Hell Mouth, the Hell Mouth: The Hell Mouth closes it is closed. So it is and will be.

END MUSIC

We all of us make mistakes but just think of what it would be like to understand another person's mistakes: and not present or past ones but future ones. The truth is that knowing what mistakes they will make will help them be their mistakes and not yours and of course you may even be able to capitalize upon their failures.

Vine magick to get knowledge of future mistakes of a chosen person

(You will need the music Night Fever by The Bee Gees, ready to start: any adverts before music should be listened to already)

MUSIC PLAYING: NIGHT FEVER MOVE TO THE MUSIC AS YOU SAY THESE WORDS

Leviathan you are a powerful devil a great monster and your mouth is the very mouth of Hell itself. Leviathan powerful devil and I ask

that you open your mouth that is the very mouth of Hell itself: The

Gates of Hell, the Hell Mouth. Leviathan open the Hell Mouth, the

Hell Mouth: The Hell Mouth opens it is open. I summon through

the Hell Mouth the King and Earl and of Hell, Vine, he who is the

lion holding the snake, while riding a black horse, commander of

36 legions of demons. Vine come through the gates: Vine comes

through the gates and is here with me. Vine King of Hell I ask that

you make it so that your 36 legions give me knowledge of the

future mistakes of state name of chosen person and this is what I

ask of you. Vine King of Hell agrees to help and departs back

through the Mouth of Hell. Leviathan you are a powerful devil a

great monster and your mouth is the very mouth of Hell itself.

Leviathan powerful devil and I ask that you close your mouth that

is the very mouth of Hell itself: The Gates of Hell, the Hell Mouth.

Leviathan close the Hell Mouth, the Hell Mouth: The Hell Mouth closes it is closed. So it is and will be.

END MUSIC

The magick you will learn now is to give information that is about any organization of your choosing. Organizations run on knowledge as much as they do people and money. However, I know that in reality the truth is that in life knowing about an organization can help you get employed, simply be better informed and even make you rich. This magick now follows.

Vine magick to get knowledge of a chosen organization

(You will need the music Funkytown by Lipps Inc.: any adverts before music should be listened to already)

MUSIC PLAYING: FUNKYTOWN MOVE TO THE MUSIC AS YOU SAY THESE WORDS

Leviathan you are a powerful devil a great monster and your mouth is the very mouth of Hell itself. Leviathan powerful devil and I ask

that you open your mouth that is the very mouth of Hell itself: The Gates of Hell, the Hell Mouth. Leviathan open the Hell Mouth, the Hell Mouth: The Hell Mouth opens it is open. I summon through the Hell Mouth the King and Earl and of Hell, Vine, he who is the lion holding the snake, while riding a black horse, commander of 36 legions of demons. Vine come through the gates: Vine comes through the gates and is here with me. Vine King of Hell I ask that you make it so that your 36 legions give hidden knowledge of the organization state name of chosen organization and this is what I ask of you. Vine King of Hell agrees to help and departs back through the Mouth of Hell. Leviathan you are a powerful devil a great monster and your mouth is the very mouth of Hell itself. Leviathan powerful devil and I ask that you close your mouth that is the very mouth of Hell itself: The Gates of Hell, the Hell Mouth. Leviathan close the Hell Mouth, the Hell Mouth: The Hell Mouth closes it is closed. So it is and will be.

END MUSIC

You have now learnt a good array of magick that uses the entity known as Vine. I feel that this helps us to know that there exist things outside of our daily experience and these things may not even be of this world. However this does not diminish our ability to function in the mundanity of the modern world but helps us because we understand that of the many ways our world could have been put together this is one choice only and yet I feel that in many ways it is probably the best one for our particular jigsaw puzzle. I think we should appreciate the world and what it does and what is within it besides ourselves. Surely anyone who can work this magick must be able to do wonderful things if they only try.

Chapter 5 Eligos for power

Eligos is a Grand Duke of Hell itself and we shall be using him and his 60 legions that he commands to assist us in matters related to power: and power itself. Power should never be forgotten because without it, life is almost intolerable and everything is more difficult. However, when we discover no usual options, we should not forget that we always have magick.

Eligos magick for more power

(You will need the music I will survive by, Gloria Gaynor: any adverts before music should be listened to already)

MUSIC PLAYING: I WILL SURVIVE MOVE TO THE MUSIC AS YOU SAY THESE WORDS

Leviathan you are a powerful devil a great monster and your mouth is the very mouth of Hell itself. Leviathan powerful devil and I ask that you open your mouth that is the very mouth of Hell itself: The

Gates of Hell, the Hell Mouth. Leviathan open the Hell Mouth, the Hell Mouth: The Hell Mouth opens it is open. I summon through the Hell Mouth the Grand Duke of Hell, Eligos, the knight riding a horse, he with 60 legions of demons at his command. Eligos come through the gates: Eligos comes through the gates and is here with me. Eligos Grand Duke of Hell I ask that you make it so that your 60 legions will make me more powerful and this is what I ask of you. Eligos the Grand Duke of Hell agrees to help and departs back through the Mouth of Hell. Leviathan you are a powerful devil a great monster and your mouth is the very mouth of Hell itself. Leviathan powerful devil and I ask that you close your mouth that is the very mouth of Hell itself: The Gates of Hell, the Hell Mouth. Leviathan close the Hell Mouth, the Hell Mouth: The Hell Mouth closes it is closed. So it is and will be.

END MUSIC

I feel that the most important form of power isn't about having inner power or power over ourselves but power over other people. Indeed, this is why I now offer you magic you will have this most important form of power and this is what I feel makes this next magick important. However, there is always choice and so you maybe choose to use this following magick or not. I am not a maker of slaves I would rather free them all and maybe then slave masters would never walk the Earth again.

Eligos magick for power over many people

(You will need the music Ma Baker by, Boney M: any adverts before music should be listened to already)

MUSIC PLAYING: MA BAKER MOVE TO THE MUSIC AS YOU SAY THESE WORDS

Leviathan you are a powerful devil a great monster and your mouth is the very mouth of Hell itself. Leviathan powerful devil and I ask

that you open your mouth that is the very mouth of Hell itself: The Gates of Hell, the Hell Mouth. Leviathan open the Hell Mouth, the Hell Mouth: The Hell Mouth opens it is open. I summon through the Hell Mouth the Grand Duke of Hell, Eligos, the knight riding a horse, he with 60 legions of demons at his command. Eligos come through the gates: Eligos comes through the gates and is here with me. Eligos Grand Duke of Hell I ask that you make it so that your 60 legions will give me power over lots of people and this is what I ask of you. Eligos the Grand Duke of Hell agrees to help and departs back through the Mouth of Hell. Leviathan you are a powerful devil a great monster and your mouth is the very mouth of Hell itself. Leviathan powerful devil and I ask that you close your mouth that is the very mouth of Hell itself: The Gates of Hell, the Hell Mouth. Leviathan close the Hell Mouth, the Hell Mouth: The Hell Mouth closes it is closed. So it is and will be.

END MUSIC

Material success is in fact wealth and having lots of it. Of course, it is true that there are other forms of material success and abundance is part of this too. But this magick will help you to gain what you desire and need. I know that life isn't always easy but also know that this magick can assist you to gain a better life and make things materially easier for you.

Eligos magick for material success

(You will need the music Le Freak, by Chic: any adverts before music should be listened to already)

MUSIC PLAYING: LE FREAK MOVE TO THE MUSIC AS YOU SAY THESE WORDS

Leviathan you are a powerful devil a great monster and your mouth is the very mouth of Hell itself. Leviathan powerful devil and I ask that you open your mouth that is the very mouth of Hell itself: The Gates of Hell, the Hell Mouth. Leviathan open the Hell Mouth, the

Hell Mouth: The Hell Mouth opens it is open. I summon through the Hell Mouth the Grand Duke of Hell, Eligos, the knight riding a horse, he with 60 legions of demons at his command. Eligos come through the gates: Eligos comes through the gates and is here with me. Eligos Grand Duke of Hell I ask that you make it so that your 60 legions will help me be successful in financial matters and materially in all ways and this is what I ask of you. Eligos the Grand Duke of Hell agrees to help and departs back through the Mouth of Hell. Leviathan you are a powerful devil a great monster and your mouth is the very mouth of Hell itself. Leviathan powerful devil and I ask that you close your mouth that is the very mouth of Hell itself: The Gates of Hell, the Hell Mouth. Leviathan close the Hell Mouth, the Hell Mouth: The Hell Mouth closes it is closed. So it is and will be.

END MUSIC

We all have enemies and usually rivals even if we are not aware of it. The truth is that some people choose to live their lives in hate and this may make them dangerous to you. In many ways our emotional state is more important than our physical one or even our apparent success. However, enemies and rivals are concepts as much as anything and this ironically gives them greater power and makes them problems, I feel you must be prepared to deal with: but you decide what is right in your life. This magick follows now.

Eligos magick for victory over all enemies and rivals

(You will need the music Voulez-Vou, by Abba: any adverts before music should be listened to already)

MUSIC PLAYING: VOULEZ-VOU MOVE TO THE MUSIC AS YOU SAY THESE WORDS

Leviathan you are a powerful devil a great monster and your mouth is the very mouth of Hell itself. Leviathan powerful devil and I ask

that you open your mouth that is the very mouth of Hell itself: The Gates of Hell, the Hell Mouth. Leviathan open the Hell Mouth, the Hell Mouth: The Hell Mouth opens it is open. I summon through the Hell Mouth the Grand Duke of Hell, Eligos, the knight riding a horse, he with 60 legions of demons at his command. Eligos come through the gates: Eligos comes through the gates and is here with me. Eligos Grand Duke of Hell I ask that you make it so that your 60 legions will make me victorious over all enemies and rivals and this is what I ask of you. Eligos the Grand Duke of Hell agrees to help and departs back through the Mouth of Hell. Leviathan you are a powerful devil a great monster and your mouth is the very mouth of Hell itself. Leviathan powerful devil and I ask that you close your mouth that is the very mouth of Hell itself: The Gates of Hell, the Hell Mouth. Leviathan close the Hell Mouth, the Hell Mouth: The Hell Mouth closes it is closed. So it is and will be.

END MUSIC

You have now read and hopefully worked some of this potent magick. The truth is that in life we often must leave some problems aside if we do not have magick. However, I feel that magick is best used alongside the mundane non-magical if we can. It is best not simply to replace one form of effort: the non-magical: with another: the magical: when we can and should be using both together one complimenting the other. When we do this, we gain a greater power because often the most successful use all forms of power they have at their disposal and when they do this, they are more likely to win then they would otherwise. This is also helpful because power of any sort often helps us acquire power of other sorts increasing the power, we possess overall.

Chapter 6 Eligos protection and strategy

Strategy is often that which is the difference between success and total failure and in a world where sometimes failure is death, we need to understand strategy. Eligos can help you to understand strategy and so with this in mind I offer magick to help you: and here it is.

Eligos magick to help you understand strategy

(You will need the music Night Fever by, the Bee Gees: any adverts before music should be listened to already)

MUSIC PLAYING: NIGHT FEVER MOVE TO THE MUSIC AS YOU SAY THESE WORDS

Leviathan you are a powerful devil a great monster and your mouth is the very mouth of Hell itself. Leviathan powerful devil and I ask that you open your mouth that is the very mouth of Hell itself: The Gates of Hell, the Hell Mouth. Leviathan open the Hell Mouth, the

46

Hell Mouth: The Hell Mouth opens it is open. I summon through the Hell Mouth the Grand Duke of Hell, Eligos, the knight riding a horse, he with 60 legions of demons at his command. Eligos come through the gates: Eligos comes through the gates and is here with me. Eligos Grand Duke of Hell I ask that you help me understand strategy and this is what I ask of you. Eligos the Grand Duke of Hell agrees to help and departs back through the Mouth of Hell. Leviathan you are a powerful devil a great monster and your mouth is the very mouth of Hell itself. Leviathan powerful devil and I ask that you close your mouth that is the very mouth of Hell itself: The Gates of Hell, the Hell Mouth. Leviathan close the Hell Mouth, the Hell Mouth: The Hell Mouth closes it is closed. So it is and will be. END MUSIC

Wars are the largest and best example of violence. But there are many types of wars and alongside the bold and obvious wars there are cold wars and wars we fight sometimes against some aspect of ourselves and even against addictions. Maybe this is why the concept of war never stops and so we must win because to lose a war is often death and this is something we should forestall for as long ae we can.

Eligos magick to win any wars

(You will need the music I will survive by, Gloria Gaynor: any adverts before music should be listened to already)

MUSIC PLAYING: I WILL SURVIVE MOVE TO THE MUSIC AS YOU SAY THESE WORDS

Leviathan you are a powerful devil a great monster and your mouth is the very mouth of Hell itself. Leviathan powerful devil and I ask that you open your mouth that is the very mouth of Hell itself: The Gates of Hell, the Hell Mouth. Leviathan open the Hell Mouth, the Hell Mouth: The Hell Mouth opens it is open. I summon through the Hell Mouth the Grand Duke of Hell, Eligos, the knight riding a horse, he with 60 legions of demons at his command. Eligos come through the gates: Eligos comes through the gates and is here with me. Eligos Grand Duke of Hell I ask that you make it so that your 60 legions will help me to win any wars and this is what I ask of you. Eligos the Grand Duke of Hell agrees to help and departs back through the Mouth of Hell. Leviathan you are a powerful devil a great monster and your mouth is the very mouth of Hell itself. Leviathan powerful devil and I ask that you close your mouth that is the very mouth of Hell itself: The Gates of Hell, the Hell Mouth. Leviathan close the Hell Mouth, the Hell Mouth: The Hell Mouth closes it is closed. So it is and will be.

END MUSIC

We should all have protection because we may get attacked and so need it. It is best however to get protection before you are likely to need it: at the first opportunity in fact. This next magick is for protection and although it is strongest against curses and all manner of magical attacks, it still has some power against physical ones.

Eligos magick for protection

(You will need the music, You should be dancing by the Bee Gees: any adverts before music should be listened to already)

MUSIC PLAYING: YOU SHOULD BE DANCING MOVE TO THE MUSIC AS YOU SAY THESE WORDS

Leviathan you are a powerful devil a great monster and your mouth is the very mouth of Hell itself. Leviathan powerful devil and I ask that you open your mouth that is the very mouth of Hell itself: The Gates of Hell, the Hell Mouth. Leviathan open the Hell Mouth, the Hell Mouth: The Hell Mouth opens it is open. I summon through the Hell Mouth the Grand Duke of Hell, Eligos, the knight riding a horse, he with 60 legions of demons at his command. Eligos come through the gates: Eligos comes through the gates and is here with me. Eligos Grand Duke of Hell I ask that you make it so that your 60 legions will protect me from all harm and this is what I ask of you. Eligos the Grand Duke of Hell agrees to help and departs back through the Mouth of Hell. Leviathan you are a powerful devil a great monster and your mouth is the very mouth of Hell itself. Leviathan powerful devil and I ask that you close your mouth that is the very mouth of Hell itself: The Gates of Hell, the Hell Mouth. Leviathan close the Hell Mouth, the Hell Mouth: The Hell Mouth closes it is closed. So it is and will be.

END MUSIC

It is generally the case that we wish to protect those we are close to and this includes our friends and family. In fact, this is the reason for this next magick. However, I understand that in life we sometimes get pulled into other people's problems and so protecting those you are near to and care about will in turn make your life easier.

Eligos magick to protect your friends and family

(You will need the music Funkytown, by Lipps Inc: any adverts before music should be listened to already)

MUSIC PLAYING: SEPTEMBER MOVE TO THE MUSIC AS YOU SAY THESE WORDS

Leviathan you are a powerful devil a great monster and your mouth is the very mouth of Hell itself. Leviathan powerful devil and I ask that you open your mouth that is the very mouth of Hell itself: The Gates of Hell, the Hell Mouth. Leviathan open the Hell Mouth, the Hell Mouth: The Hell Mouth opens it is open. I summon through the Hell Mouth the Grand Duke of Hell, Eligos, the knight riding a horse, he with 60 legions of demons at his command. Eligos come through the gates: Eligos comes through the gates and is here with me. Eligos Grand Duke of Hell I ask that you make it so that your 60 legions will protect myself and my friends and family and this is what I ask of you. Eligos the Grand Duke of Hell agrees to help and departs back through the Mouth of Hell. Leviathan you are a powerful devil a great monster and your mouth is the very mouth of Hell itself. Leviathan powerful devil and I ask that you close your mouth that is the very mouth of Hell itself: The Gates of Hell, the Hell Mouth. Leviathan close the Hell Mouth, the Hell Mouth: The Hell Mouth closes it is closed. So it is and will be.

END MUSIC

You have now expanded the range of power than you had: you have become stronger. This book helps people to gain more tools they may utilize in their lives. I feel the best magick is the magick you will use and in truth this magick here is all useful and even the music may be gotten from playing YouTube or some other video or music sharing site, so do not imagine that everything here is difficult because of the added aspect of music. In fact, this music greatly adds to the potency of the magick that is here. But more than that this music helps to give an extra feeling to this magick

because it helps us be more aggressive yet also positive and upbeat

and this is a difficult think to achieve with satanic magick.

Chapter 7 Bathin travel

Bathin is a devil with power over travel and crystals and herbs. However, this sounds rather tame until we really understand his power through experience and this is that Bathin can instantly physically transport anyone anywhere. This means he could send you from where you are now to anywhere on Earth and beyond. However, do bear in mind that in reality this magick does not always work: it is difficult magick. But if it does not seem to work Bathin will do whatever he needs to get you: or anyone else that is the target of this magick: to get there via mundane means such as a flight. This means never work magick using Bathin to somewhere you wouldn't want the expense of a holiday because if it doesn't work you will end up going there anyway because he may hound you until you do. Bathin is a Great Duke and so has great power. I hope this small warning helps you understand that this magick is not to be messed with it needs to be done with care when you really want it to work. However, using it on others as a curse is a different thing altogether.

Bathin magick to protect send your enemies to a country of your choosing

(You will need the music Hot stuff by Donna Summers: any adverts before music should be listened to already)

MUSIC PLAYING: HOT STUFF MOVE TO THE MUSIC AS YOU SAY THESE WORDS

Leviathan you are a powerful devil a great monster and your mouth is the very mouth of Hell itself. Leviathan powerful devil and I ask that you open your mouth that is the very mouth of Hell itself: The Gates of Hell, the Hell Mouth. Leviathan open the Hell Mouth, the Hell Mouth: The Hell Mouth opens it is open. I summon through the Hell Mouth the Great Duke of Hell, Bathin, the strongman with a serpentine tail riding a pale horse, he with 30 legions of demons at his command. Bathin come through the gates: Bathin comes through the gates and is here with me. Bathin Great Duke of Hell I ask that you send my enemies to <u>state name of country you wish them to go</u> and this is what I ask of you. Bathin the Great Duke of Hell agrees to help and departs back through the Mouth of Hell. Leviathan you are a powerful devil a great monster and your mouth is the very mouth of Hell itself. Leviathan powerful devil and I ask that you close your mouth that is the very mouth of Hell itself: The Gates of Hell, the Hell Mouth. Leviathan close the Hell Mouth, the Hell Mouth: The Hell Mouth closes it is closed. So it is and will be. END MUSIC

By cautious with this magick by only using it to be places you really want to be and also carry a passport while working it if uncertain of getting back. However certainly have within your wallet or purse the spell that got you there for return travelling. Maybe chose short journeys like places near home first.

Bathin magick to be transported to a location of your choosing

(You will need the music You should be dancing by the Bee Gees: any adverts before music should be listened to already)

MUSIC PLAYING: YOU SHOULD BE DANCING MOVE TO THE MUSIC AS YOU SAY THESE WORDS

Leviathan you are a powerful devil a great monster and your mouth is the very mouth of Hell itself. Leviathan powerful devil and I ask that you open your mouth that is the very mouth of Hell itself: The Gates of Hell, the Hell Mouth. Leviathan open the Hell Mouth, the Hell Mouth: The Hell Mouth opens it is open. I summon through the Hell Mouth the Great Duke of Hell, Bathin, the strongman with a serpentine tail riding a pale horse, he with 30 legions of demons at his command. Bathin come through the gates: Bathin comes through the gates and is here with me. Bathin Great Duke of Hell I ask that you transport me instantly to state chosen location and this

58

is what I ask of you. Bathin the Great Duke of Hell agrees to help and departs back through the Mouth of Hell. Leviathan you are a powerful devil a great monster and your mouth is the very mouth of Hell itself. Leviathan powerful devil and I ask that you close your mouth that is the very mouth of Hell itself: The Gates of Hell, the Hell Mouth. Leviathan close the Hell Mouth, the Hell Mouth: The Hell Mouth closes it is closed. So it is and will be.

END MUSIC

With this magick it is best to try and pick somewhere unpleasant for them to be. However, unless you leave them in a desert without water people have this nasty habit of coming back. Use this magick while willing it to work and your chances are greatly increased.

Bathin magick to transport your rivals to somewhere of your choice

(You will need the music Hot stuff by Donna Summers: any adverts before music should be listened to already)

MUSIC PLAYING: HOT STUFF MOVE TO THE MUSIC AS YOU SAY THESE WORDS

Leviathan you are a powerful devil a great monster and your mouth is the very mouth of Hell itself. Leviathan powerful devil and I ask that you open your mouth that is the very mouth of Hell itself: The Gates of Hell, the Hell Mouth. Leviathan open the Hell Mouth, the Hell Mouth: The Hell Mouth opens it is open. I summon through the Hell Mouth the Great Duke of Hell, Bathin, the strongman with a serpentine tail riding a pale horse, he with 30 legions of demons at his command. Bathin come through the gates: Bathin comes through the gates and is here with me. Bathin Great Duke of Hell I

ask that you transport my rivals to <u>state name of the location you</u> <u>want them transported to</u> and this is what I ask of you. Bathin the Great Duke of Hell agrees to help and departs back through the Mouth of Hell. Leviathan you are a powerful devil a great monster and your mouth is the very mouth of Hell itself. Leviathan powerful devil and I ask that you close your mouth that is the very mouth of Hell itself: The Gates of Hell, the Hell Mouth. Leviathan close the Hell Mouth, the Hell Mouth: The Hell Mouth closes it is closed. So it is and will be.

END MUSIC

The following magick is in a way protective magick in that it sends attackers away and this will certainly make them think before even thinking of attacking you again. But this magick is your choice as to whether you work it or not: freedom of choice and freewill are important to me, I am no slave maker I wish to free the slaves.

Bathin magick to send all attackers far away

(You will need the music Dancing queen by Abba: any adverts before music should be listened to already)

MUSIC PLAYING: DANCING QUEEN MOVE TO THE MUSIC AS YOU SAY THESE WORDS

Leviathan you are a powerful devil a great monster and your mouth is the very mouth of Hell itself. Leviathan powerful devil and I ask that you open your mouth that is the very mouth of Hell itself: The Gates of Hell, the Hell Mouth. Leviathan open the Hell Mouth, the Hell Mouth: The Hell Mouth opens it is open. I summon through the Hell Mouth the Great Duke of Hell, Bathin, the strongman with a serpentine tail riding a pale horse, he with 30 legions of demons at his command. Bathin come through the gates: Bathin comes through the gates and is here with me. Bathin Great Duke of Hell I ask that you send all attackers far away and this is what I ask of you. Bathin the Great Duke of Hell agrees to help and departs back through the Mouth of Hell. Leviathan you are a powerful devil a great monster and your mouth is the very mouth of Hell itself. Leviathan powerful devil and I ask that you close your mouth that is the very mouth of Hell itself: The Gates of Hell, the Hell Mouth. Leviathan close the Hell Mouth, the Hell Mouth: The Hell Mouth closes it is closed. So it is and will be.

END MUSIC

Astral projection is safer than actual travel and some people can see astral bodies while some can't. The truth is that astral projection is usually not that accurate and it is usually more like a dream mixed in with some truth. I suppose we should be glad for what we have and this following magick will make this magical skill easier.

Bathin magick to be able to see other places through astral projection

(You will need the music Boogie Wonderland by Earth, wind and fire: any adverts before music should be listened to already)

MUSIC PLAYING: HOT STUFF MOVE TO THE MUSIC AS YOU SAY THESE WORDS

Leviathan you are a powerful devil a great monster and your mouth is the very mouth of Hell itself. Leviathan powerful devil and I ask that you open your mouth that is the very mouth of Hell itself: The Gates of Hell, the Hell Mouth. Leviathan open the Hell Mouth, the Hell Mouth: The Hell Mouth opens it is open. I summon through the Hell Mouth the Great Duke of Hell, Bathin, the strongman with a serpentine tail riding a pale horse, he with 30 legions of demons at his command. Bathin come through the gates: Bathin comes through the gates and is here with me. Bathin Great Duke of Hell I

ask that you give me the gift of astral projection and this is what I ask of you. Bathin the Great Duke of Hell agrees to help and departs back through the Mouth of Hell. Leviathan you are a powerful devil a great monster and your mouth is the very mouth of Hell itself. Leviathan powerful devil and I ask that you close your mouth that is the very mouth of Hell itself: The Gates of Hell, the Hell Mouth. Leviathan close the Hell Mouth, the Hell Mouth: The Hell Mouth closes it is closed. So it is and will be.

END MUSIC

You have gained a lot of knowledge and now know of Bathin. However, there is more magick to come you have not finished yet. But soon the full range of magick that is here shall be yours.

Chapter 8 Bathin success and victory

This chapter in many ways concentrated on success and victory and related concepts. In fact, success and victory are not enemies to him he has both in abundance and this is partly due to the 30 legions of demons he has under his control. But this magick still requires a powerful will for it to work: but will it to work and it shall.

Bathin magick to use his 30 legions to make you more successful

(You will need the music Mamma Mia by Abba; any adverts before music should be listened to already)

MUSIC PLAYING: HOT STUFF MOVE TO THE MUSIC AS YOU SAY THESE WORDS

Leviathan you are a powerful devil a great monster and your mouth is the very mouth of Hell itself. Leviathan powerful devil and I ask

that you open your mouth that is the very mouth of Hell itself: The Gates of Hell, the Hell Mouth. Leviathan open the Hell Mouth, the Hell Mouth: The Hell Mouth opens it is open. I summon through the Hell Mouth the Great Duke of Hell, Bathin, the strongman with a serpentine tail riding a pale horse, he with 30 legions of demons at his command. Bathin come through the gates: Bathin comes through the gates and is here with me. Bathin Great Duke of Hell I ask that you use your powers and your 30 legions of demons to make me more successful and this is what I ask of you. Bathin the Great Duke of Hell agrees to help and departs back through the Mouth of Hell. Leviathan you are a powerful devil a great monster and your mouth is the very mouth of Hell itself. Leviathan powerful devil and I ask that you close your mouth that is the very mouth of Hell itself: The Gates of Hell, the Hell Mouth. Leviathan close the Hell Mouth, the Hell Mouth: The Hell Mouth closes it is closed. So it is and will be.

END MUSIC

We all have enemies even if we do not know who they are and also rivals and problems occur in the lives of us all. In many ways the true test of us is how we are able to deal with difficulties not how many times they occur or how bad. This means that the following magick is useful because it helps you have the positive side of victory in your life: magick follows.

Bathin magick to give you victory over all enemies, rivals and problems

(You will need the music YMCA by the Village People; any adverts before music should be listened to already)

MUSIC PLAYING: YMCA MOVE TO THE MUSIC AS YOU SAY THESE WORDS

Leviathan you are a powerful devil a great monster and your mouth is the very mouth of Hell itself. Leviathan powerful devil and I ask that you open your mouth that is the very mouth of Hell itself: The Gates of Hell, the Hell Mouth. Leviathan open the Hell Mouth, the Hell Mouth: The Hell Mouth opens it is open. I summon through the Hell Mouth the Great Duke of Hell, Bathin, the strongman with a serpentine tail riding a pale horse, he with 30 legions of demons at his command. Bathin come through the gates: Bathin comes through the gates and is here with me. Bathin Great Duke of Hell I ask that you use your powers and your 30 legions of demons to make me victorious over all enemies, rivals and problems and this is what I ask of you. Bathin the Great Duke of Hell agrees to help and departs back through the Mouth of Hell. Leviathan you are a powerful devil a great monster and your mouth is the very mouth of Hell itself. Leviathan powerful devil and I ask that you close your mouth that is the very mouth of Hell itself: The Gates of Hell, the

Hell Mouth. Leviathan close the Hell Mouth, the Hell Mouth: The Hell Mouth closes it is closed. So it is and will be.

END MUSIC

For some people greater power is their main aim in life. In fact, this is not as poor a choice as it may seem because power prevents us from being enslaved and protects us from other threats and gives us that most wonderful of things, choice. I understand that power they say corrupts and maybe it does but this only helps us understand that the best person to possess power is you because these things are only the problem of other people. Meaning if you are corrupted you because a corrupt powerful person that makes other peoples lives bad whereas when it is someone else your life is one of those being made bad. This magick is the last in the book and yet you may choose not to use it if you desire: why you would do this I cannot imagine but it is your choice.

Bathin magick to use his 30 legions to make you more powerful

(You will need the music Ma Baker by Boney M; any adverts before music should be listened to already)

MUSIC PLAYING: HOT STUFF MOVE TO THE MUSIC AS YOU SAY THESE WORDS

Leviathan you are a powerful devil a great monster and your mouth is the very mouth of Hell itself. Leviathan powerful devil and I ask that you open your mouth that is the very mouth of Hell itself: The Gates of Hell, the Hell Mouth. Leviathan open the Hell Mouth, the Hell Mouth: The Hell Mouth opens it is open. I summon through the Hell Mouth the Great Duke of Hell, Bathin, the strongman with a serpentine tail riding a pale horse, he with 30 legions of demons at his command. Bathin come through the gates: Bathin comes through the gates and is here with me. Bathin Great Duke of Hell I

ask that you use your powers and your 30 legions of demons to make me more powerful, left power of all forms be mine and this is what I ask of you. Bathin the Great Duke of Hell agrees to help and departs back through the Mouth of Hell. Leviathan you are a powerful devil a great monster and your mouth is the very mouth of Hell itself. Leviathan powerful devil and I ask that you close your mouth that is the very mouth of Hell itself: The Gates of Hell, the Hell Mouth. Leviathan close the Hell Mouth, the Hell Mouth: The Hell Mouth closes it is closed. So it is and will be.

END MUSIC

You have now come to understand this magick: this magick within these pages. You are more powerful than you were and a greater, more powerful person than you were and yet still the same you. In many ways this magick is not unlike the clothes we wear; the knowledge is with us like clothes are as we walk around this world. In fact, magick was always within you but without some knowledge there was no way to utilize it no matter how hard you tried. This is what separates the occultist from everyone else: they have the knowledge they do not even know to seek. Walk with pride you are an occultist.

www.ingramcontent.com/pod-product-compliance
Lightning Source LLC
Chambersburg PA
CBHW070024110426
42741CB00034B/2470